IT Management for *Little** Companies

*From one-person shops
to just too small to have
Information Technology staff

Margaret Chock, PhD, CMC

IT Management for
*Little**
Companies
*From one-person shops
to just too small to have
Information Technology staff

ISBN: 9798647953315

Imprint: emerson books

Table of Contents

To my husband, Ernest

Where This Book Is Coming From

Target Audience

If you're a well-trained Information Technology manager, this book might not be what you're looking for. It's aimed more at very small businesses or nonprofits which are either just getting organized, or just realizing that their computer systems are a horrible mess.

But if you're an IT manager about to face dealing with that mess, it might give you some ideas about where to get started!

Very New or Very Small Organization—No Time for IT

When you're starting a new organization, usually the last thing you have time to worry about is the computer systems that will support it.

Higher priorities include:

- How will you produce your product or service?

- Who's going to buy it? How can you sell to them? Will they pay enough to cover your production costs and keep you in business?

- Where can you get the money to get started before you're selling enough to support the organization?

- Can you defend against competitors with trade secret, copyright, or patent protection, or at least get a head start on them?

- If you can't do it all yourself, who do you need to help you? Can you afford what it will take to attract them?

You might not be able to afford a proper Information Technology manager on the payroll, or even anyone who knows much about computers.

Even if your business is in technology, the focus of your computer-savvy staff will primarily be on your products and services, rather than the tech to manage it. Even worse, such product developers may have very odd ideas about solving IT management problems that can't easily be challenged by someone of lesser technical knowledge. For instance, I know someone who wrote a payroll system for his company in APL. APL is a very concise, elegant programming language, yet it can seem indecipherable, even to its author. Days later, this programmer couldn't figure out what he had written, and the system had to be discarded very quickly.

But You Need IT

But proper management of Information Technology can give you a lot of advantages, some obvious, some less so, for handling details so you can focus on the important stuff—getting funding, finding customers, manufacturing your product or providing your service.

Solving those problems gets you deep into technology these days:

- There's the obvious—it provides all sorts of tools to do the work, to produce the product or service.
- It supports your research on
  - o Customers.
  - o Funding sources.
  - o Intellectual property issues—possibly competing patents, copyrights, and existing products/services.
  - o Staffing issues: job descriptions for clues to the skills you'll need; finding candidates or recruiting agencies.
- It provides your face to the outside world— attracting and reassuring customers and investors.

My Experience — and How It Might be Useful to You

I've been in the Information Technology field for more than 50 years (because finding out the things you can do with a computer's help is more fun than anything else out there!). Much of that time I've worked with very small companies, in some cases as their first IT professional.

My first exposure to computers was in the ancient days. My father (at various times a mining, mechanical, nuclear, electrical, biomedical and civil engineer) took me to work once, and showed me what looked like a desk-sized, metal gray box. In fact, it was a machine that they'd trained to whistle "Row, Row, Row Your Boat"!

I wasn't much impressed. Then in high school our class experienced the ENIAC computer while on a tour of Caltech—being confronted with a roomful of single-story metal panels, with switches, lights, wires, and electrical appendages galore. That was a bit impressive.

But it wasn't until my senior year of college, in Advanced Archaeology class, that I really got hooked. We learned about a study of potsherds (little broken pieces of pottery) in which the archaeologists used a computer for statistical analysis of enough data to show convincingly that such artifacts could be used to reveal social patterns. For instance, it was known somehow that in this region women made the pottery, using methods they learned from their mothers.

If all the pottery in a village had consistent sets of patterns over time, it was clear that the women lived there most of their lives; men came in as husbands, but didn't much disturb the pottery industry. But where there was a varying assortment of pot designs, women were the ones on the move, bringing their diverse traditions to daily life in their husbands' villages. All that insight from using a computer. I thought that was the neatest thing!

Immediately after graduation I started looking for computer-related jobs. Not finding any available to women in the local area (I had just married a graduate student who was tied to his laboratory in the middle of working on his degree), I went back to school to finish a second major in mathematics. At this point I finally found a low-level job as a Technical Computer (somebody who was supposed to do math calculations and draw graphs by hand—*Hidden Figures* is a good movie about women like that). I was lucky enough to have a manager who gave me some actual computer projects—FORTRAN calculations on an old IBM 704 mainframe with vacuum tubes that blew every 10 minutes, and BASIC operations on their pioneering online system using paper tape.

Lessons learned:

◆ Back up your data—*quick*—before it evaporates!

◆ If a faraway computer is working on your application, it can take a long time to respond, and you're dependent on the communication channel working to get any response at all.

◆ If you're submitting your program and data on punched cards, use the last 8 columns for sequence numbers. Otherwise you are in real trouble if you drop the box and the cards get mixed up.

After several months I realized that it took the last woman with my capabilities five years to gain recognition (and pay) as a professional staff member. Since my husband's advisor had finally signed off on his dissertation, I broadened my job search to the big city, and landed a real programming job with Computer Usage Development Corp., a pioneering software house with respect for women's technical capabilities.

CUDC trained me to write software in IBM Basic Assembly Language, and how to identify the various airplanes landing at the international airport across the road by their logos. Then after a couple of weeks they sent me to JPL—not as a scientific programmer based on my science background and training in FORTRAN for engineering, but as a COBOL applications programmer for a cost accounting system. As my "training," my supervisor handed me two densely packed, inch-thick manuals, and said, "Here. Learn COBOL."

Lesson learned:

◆ When you've seen three computer languages, you've seen them all.

I learned COBOL, and vicariously learned systems analysis. Our analyst was fresh out of graduate school, and had developed a beautiful set of cost estimation forms and reports in black, white, and multiple shades of green. However, placement of the data on the various forms and reports required re-sorting it at nearly every step. JPL's business mainframe computer stored its data on magnetic tape, so each sort required numerous reads and writes of the data tapes.

The entire process took longer than a day, which didn't work well for the daily reports, to say nothing of their weekly and monthly summaries. We also had to wait up to a week to get our tests run, though I found that by driving in at 2 AM to start the workday I could sometimes squeeze jobs in during slack periods.

Lessons learned:

◆ Don't bite off more than you can chew.

◆ If you're working with a 64,000-byte memory (1 byte being the equivalent of an alphabetic character; for reference, my current laptop has a 16,000,000,000-byte memory) and need to save space by using just 2 digits to specify the year, you'll get in trouble someday (though at this point "someday" was several decades away, and we assumed the software would have been rewritten by then).

◆ Understand the limitations of the technology you're working with.

After a couple of years, CUDC's business was slacking off; despite offers from JPL to join them as either a scientific or business programmer, I decided I was tired of the long daily commute. So I quit, had a couple of babies, and went back to school.

I got a Master's and a PhD in Computer Science from the UCLA School of Engineering, picking up a lot of in-depth understanding of how computers and software work. In one notable lecture, our enthusiastic professor described how someday soon we'd be able to hook up a keyboard and TV to a small computer so that everybody could have their own. My father acquired his, an IMSAI 8080, a few months later.

As part of my PhD thesis, I developed a nifty approach to dealing with massive amounts of geographic and miscellaneous data in a variety of formats (satellite photos, city and census track boundaries and statistics, road networks, potential site locations and the like), with a simple language for doing all sorts of analysis on them. I even got someone from JPL to admit that my system could do some tricks that their competing satellite remote sensing system couldn't. I also wrote a paper explaining how the same software could be used in healthcare for studies of epidemiology and hospital design.

Just when I graduated, the Apple II became available, a personal computer that was very easy to use. It could even run a version of my software—which I'd been restricted to testing at night on UCLA's big mainframe. And I got the illusion that given the PC's capabilities I could start my own software company without having to hire any staff. Nowadays, at least in Los Angeles and other tech hubs, there are a lot of organizations and consultants ready to advise new entrepreneurs about the realities of business!

I drifted into consulting to support the business, and eventually learned enough about marketing to understand that there wasn't a big enough market for my software to support even a one-person organization.

Lesson learned:

◆ Running a small business is a lot more complicated than just managing its IT.

As a consultant, I specialized in image processing and Geographic Information Systems (GIS), usually helping civil engineering firms with projects for local government agencies. A notable project was establishing the information technology capabilities for a large port, designed around a GIS to be used as a combined facilities management/land management system. Previously they had relied on remote terminals supported by other organizations for accounting and a few engineering applications. The requirements I helped them define grew from two surveyors' workstations to a new enterprise-wide computer network. I managed it through the full development life cycle: system design, site preparation, installation, staff training, integration of legacy applications, pilot projects, several months of production use, upgrades, expansion, and establishment of an Information Systems Division, which entailed coordinating more than 30 people. Twenty years later the Information Technology Director told me they'd finally outgrown the systems I'd put in place—not to boast, but not bad for what would normally be five-year obsolescence!

Along the way I worked with several small nonprofit organizations to develop their first computer capabilities, frequently membership databases, as well as to help them select their other office management software.

After the GIS consulting market dried up, and as cities started helping each other and the engineering firms were able to hire in-house experts, I went to work for a small aerospace firm as an internal consultant. In a little over four years, while I sat at the same desk, that firm merged into a middle-sized firm, and then into the fourth-largest aerospace company in the world. Along the way I inventoried the internal business systems that came with the original firm—88 of them classified as "business critical"—and their interrelationships (or lack thereof), and also helped define the management systems to be used in what we suspected might have been the largest aerospace project ever, meeting online with proposal partners in companies all over North America and Europe.

Remember the 2-digit year I mentioned earlier? That was the basis of the Year 2000 or Y2K crisis, when computers the world over were expected to go haywire on January 1, 2000, when they would try to add 1 to 12/31/99 and fail to get 01/01/100. Six months before that event, the IT Manager for the 88 critical and a few other systems quit abruptly. I grabbed the steering wheel, and we got everything rewritten, replaced or discarded in time.

Big aerospace outsourced me to a big consulting company. The work was interesting as we transitioned the eleven independent fiefdoms of the medium-sized company into the really big one and started training staff to use consistent procedures, but then I was promoted to a group of senior project managers that had nothing to do but check off the existence of required project documents from other managers. One of my colleagues referred to it as "the worst job he ever had."

I jumped ship to a little pharmaceutical research institute that needed someone who could do both IT management and image processing research. I developed their Information Technology architecture and managed their IT, providing systems for image processing, experiment data management, and chemical library notebooks. I analyzed the process for ordering chemical reagents, and helped avoid a planned barcode system that would have been less efficient than their current manual methods.

That job was too good to be true; the institute was shut down, and the parent company sold to a big multinational.

So I went back to consulting. Some of my work has been helping small companies get organized; much of the rest has been litigation support, analyzing the mistakes that technology companies and their clients make while working together.

Altogether I've seen a lot of Information Technology operations, both large and small; developed processes and systems that worked; and seen a lot of mistakes that could have been avoided. I hope this book will be useful in keeping your technology running smoothly, so you can focus on what you really want to do!

IT Management for *Little** Companies
*From one-person shops
to just too small to have
Information Technology staff

Summary: Lessons Ahead

If you really don't have time to read this book, here's what it suggests you do based on my mistakes and other people's (some of which, fortunately, were avoided):

◆ Capture your data,
information and knowledge

◆ Be paranoid

◆ Prioritize

◆ Get organized

◆ Use software tools

◆ Get help

◆ If and when you add staff,
repeat the above…

◆ And keep repeating

IT Management for *Little** Companies
*From one-person shops
to just too small to have
Information Technology staff

One-Person Band

Much of this section is based on my own decades of experience as a (usually) one-person consulting firm, plus work with clients and other associates, many of them also very small organizations. The training and reference materials available to us were usually very specific to single software or hardware technologies, or described management of a staff of IT specialists. In this section I'll try instead to address the issues that I've found important for a one-person operation, regardless of the specific technology used. Then, a later section will expand those topics to a small staff.

Capture Your Data

No matter what kind of business you're in, a large part of your work is abstract: data, Information, knowledge, processes, systems, ideas, diagrams, numbers, notes, customer contact info, best practices, etc. Nearly all of that can and should be stuffed into a computer as a set of **documents**.

**My definition of "document":* Any computer file that contains data or information you or your organization can use. To the computer, a file is a set of data that can be named and moved around as a unit, with contents that can be understood by one or another type of computer software. Examples are Word documents, spreadsheets and PDFs.

Documents are useful for a variety of reasons:

1. Save physical space

2. Easy capture of information

3. Easy copy and share

4. Very easy search and retrieve

5. Provide building blocks to combine, recombine and build upon.

Save Physical Space

A computer makes a wonderful filing cabinet.

In my decades of business and of life I've accumulated filing cabinets and cardboard cartons full of paper—each with tidbits of valuable and interesting information I'd rarely find again even if I could remember they existed.

Now I'm spending/wasting time retroactively going back through all those papers, finding the useful sentence or two, and typing them into online documents where they're accessible.

Easy Capture

Typing a note about an idea, message, etc. into a computer can be a lot faster than handwriting—at least faster than legible handwriting in my case.

Large existing documents can be scanned, so you can read them and print copies later.

And after that you don't have to walk to the filing cabinet, find the right folder, and try to squeeze in one more sheet of paper!

Easy Copy & Share

Documents on the computer can be printed out without spending the time to leave your desk, pull them out of file drawers, and load them on a copier. And you may not even have to print them—just email them to each person who needs a copy. And let the recipients print them if they want paper!

Very Easy Search & Retrieve

Here's where computer storage really gets good.

Paper documents can only be conveniently filed by a single index—subject or date or client, etc., maybe with a sub-index that's easy to use—say different drawers for different subjects, with a file folder for each client or vendor, paperwork in the folder by date.

But when the document is on the computer, you can search by folders, sub-folders nested to any degree you like, by document title, and even by ***keywords*** (unique names, technical terms, topic headings, etc.) inside the document.

**My definition of "keyword":* A word, part of a (long) word, or phrase that's used rarely enough to be useful in a search. For instance, you probably don't use "flibbertigibbet" very often, so a search might turn up just two or three versions of a single document you used it in. "The" might turn up just about everywhere, so it won't narrow your search much.

I keep forgetting how I filed things, or what I called them—but with a few guesses at a keyword I might have used, the correct document eventually shows up.

And even physical, paper documents that must be kept for some reason can be cross-indexed to make them easy to find. Type a note on the computer to tell yourself what it is, what it looks like, where it's located.

Building Blocks

Once your data is on the computer, it's available for re-use in a variety of ways. Notes can be reorganized into marketing materials or to-do lists, by copying and pasting bits and pieces with minor rewrites.

For instance, I started this book from a set of old PowerPoint slides, moving the pieces around for a more suitable outline, changing the format, expanding the ideas, copying old notes into the document and rewriting some more (with the help of my editors) to get to what you're reading now.

Organize Your Data

Information on a computer is stored in files: collections of letters, numbers, special characters, and little pieces of information that can only be interpreted by specific pieces of software. A document is a good example—text that you can read, along with information you don't see directly that controls the formatting (font size, boldface, paragraph spacing, etc.).

In order to locate pieces of information when you need them, store them with **keywords**: words or very brief phrases you'll remember when you're looking for the information, as described in the earlier section. The most important keywords should be included in the title when possible, so they'll be easiest to find. However, it's also sometimes possible to search for files that have the keywords in the content. Best to test to make sure you have that capability before relying on it.

Keywords are also used in your website, to help the public find you through your site's content. For instance, on my site I currently use the terms "Information Technology Management," "Development Analysis & Coordination," and "Forensic Litigation Consulting" to attract potential clients needing those services.

Related files can be grouped in folders, with their own keyword names. Folders can often have named sub-folders, and sub-sub-folders when collections of files get larger or more complicated. As an example, on my computer I have folders named "Administration," "Family," one named for each active client, and "Client Archive," which is broken down into subfolders named for former clients.

I can (usually) spell, but if you can't, maybe you should keep a list of key keywords for reference. Just remember what keyword you called it.

Preserve Your Data

Back up your computer in the cloud, not just nearby. Local backup can be useful to speed things up, but ultimately, it's best to preserve your files in the digital cloud in case your office building burns down, gets flooded out, collapses in the earthquake, etc., depending on what part of the country you live in. Even data that's stored in the cloud should be backed up *elsewhere* in the cloud to make sure it doesn't exist in just one location.

According to some admittedly old statistics that are still widely quoted,* 31% of personal computer users had, at one point, experienced losing all their files. 60% of companies that lost all data closed within 6 months. 72% of companies that had major data loss disappeared within 24 months.

You need to be able to rebuild fast enough to stay in business.

In the olden days, before online backup services were readily available, a client told me about a minor disaster that could have been much worse. Burglars had broken in and stolen 32 of their 33 computers. The only thing that saved the company was that their backup computer

---

* Interactive Data Corporation statistics quoted by Marc Berthiaume, The Independent, 9/10/2008

had been malfunctioning and was lying in pieces on a worktable. The burglars didn't consider that equipment worth bothering with, so the company was able to resurrect most of its most critical data.

So back up your data and keep a copy somewhere else far away from your computers!

I use an Internet service that copies all my business files once or twice a day, without interfering with my other work. If you need a fast backup of large amounts of data, a local backup device could work faster— but then back up that device way offsite!

Develop Paranoia — and Find Out Whom to Trust!

Once your data is safely copied, start worrying about other threats beyond just losing it altogether. You risk losing your intellectual property to vandalism, theft by competitors around the world, or damage to your underlying systems.

You may need different sources of outside support for your computer hardware, software, and security. Computers crash regularly, at unfortunate times. Better to know ahead of time where to get help. Some suggestions will appear in a later section.

Thieves

If your security isn't adequate, or up-to-date enough, people will steal, vandalize, confiscate, or start misusing your information at greater and greater expense to you!

- The wrong people can get their hands on your trade secrets or other critical information.

- Computer viruses and worms can pick up credit card numbers or social security numbers— yours, or worse, your clients'.

- People can eavesdrop on your wireless network.

- The wrong parties can read your unencrypted email.

A consultant friend has found her online articles published on other consultants' websites, without attribution, and the news is full of the latest thefts of credit card and supplementary identification data.

Cybercrime

Back in the 1980s I took a class on marketing with some other information technology consultants. One of my classmates had what we considered an oddball specialty: computer security. Now with cybersecurity attacks constantly in the news headlines, he's a real celebrity!

I'd recommend immediately getting a preliminary security audit to figure out what you really need to protect, and what policies, procedures, systems, etc. are needed. And, since cybercrime is constantly evolving, an annual audit by a cybersecurity consultant with a highly-rated certification in the subject. There are a large number of organizations offering both classes and certifications, so do some research to find one that's currently highly rated.

Such an expert is likely to be expensive. I tried once to augment my PhD in Computer Science and decades of IT experience with some basic cybersecurity skills. I spent a year attending seminars from one of the professional organizations, including a two-day boot camp on the basics—and decided that I'd have to make it a full-time specialty to keep up. So don't ask me for help! Get someone well-certified who's keeping up with the field to keep your business protected. You shouldn't need much of their time, but better have them repeat the audit at least annually.

While you're waiting for your first appointment, here are a few basic steps to take to protect yourself:

- **Invest in an antivirus program:** There are a number of good options, even if they aren't perfect; get at least one, and let it update automatically to provide an inexpensive, mostly unobtrusive line of defense.

- **Look for security on websites you access:** Your browser software may have built-in security checks, or look for "https:" rather than just "http:" in the website address.

- **Test emails:** If the message from someone you know doesn't make complete sense, ask the sender whether it's legit (NOT by return email, unless you know the address).

- **Check links in emails by hovering over them before clicking:** Make sure they go to legitimate websites, the ones they claim to be, with an address structure that makes sense to you.

- **Seek out protections for hardware as well:** This includes devices for locking PCs and laptops to furniture, tracking services like

LoJack (though valuable data will probably be stolen from your hard drive before they can retrieve the device), and remote zapping apps to erase all your data from a stolen smartphone.

Legal Pitfalls

Some issues will be legal rather than technical—at this point you should also talk to your lawyer about patents, trademarks, copyrights, trade secrets, etc. to guide the security processes, as well as legal requirements for protection of clients and others.

It's helpful at this level to differentiate your IT into different components:

1. **Your core technology,** if any—lab equipment, machinery, research tools, etc. that are used to provide your organization's product or service. Make sure you have ownership or use rights, guarantees of future maintenance, adequate current infrastructure. If you can't get ownership of the software's source code and technical documentation, arrange for an escrow account—a third party that keeps current copies, and provides them to customers like

you if the vendor goes out of business. Find out if there are alternative sources for any of the capabilities. This not only protects you if the provider goes out of business or fails to support you, but also gives you a stronger hand in negotiations over price. Make sure your core and its infrastructure conform to any regulatory requirements, and will continue to do so. And make sure what you're developing won't hurt other stakeholders, like clients, investors, or the general public.

2. **Business technology**—word processors, spreadsheets, accounting packages, etc. that are needed to run nearly any business. As a one-person business, you're likely to be using fairly standard off-the-shelf products. The software is replaceable, but the data itself needs protection.

3. **Infrastructure**—telecommunications, networks, operating systems etc. that support both. Again, it's likely to be much less valuable than the core technology and your own data.

Software Malfunctions

Individual software programs can usually be fixed over the Internet. Search for the manufacturer's website first, rather than support resources—look at the name of the website rather than the heading that claims to provide help with the application. The more visible sites are usually third-party providers who'll charge for their services, and have unknown levels of capability. The manufacturer often provides decent levels of customer support. If not, then start checking the credentials of the other service providers.

Hardware Malfunctions

For hardware support, **look for services that can provide house calls.** Like cybersecurity credentials, hardware support credentials are earned through various professional associations. Search online for ratings of the credentials first, then for ratings of the local support companies. You will then have some assurance that you're getting not only well-trained advice, but that it's from someone keeping up with the fast-changing threats.

Good support may be expensive, but you won't need much of their time when your company is so small. On the other hand, it's useful to have a local service on call for support as you need it, and which may be aware of your systems and preferences from earlier visits.

Unexpected Expenses

Technology tends to come with extra expenses that aren't obvious when you buy it.

When you purchase a major piece of software, a good rule of thumb is that you'll also need to send the software vendor an additional 20% per year to get bugs fixed and keep up with the latest upgrades—you'll have to get the upgrades, or eventually the vendor won't be able to support your old version. Also, the upgrades generally include security fixes, which you'll need to protect your business.

More popular "consumer" products might rely on selling you an upgrade every few years instead. You might be able to limp along on old versions for several years, depending on which features you need, though there's a trend towards annual rentals instead.

Eventually, your upgraded software will no longer run on your old hardware, so you'll have to buy new hardware. Then some of your other old software may no longer work if you haven't kept up with the upgrades to that…it's an endless cycle.

Track the business health of your vendors carefully—
they may go out of business rather suddenly. Technology
is a volatile industry. YOU might be out of business for
days while you scramble to find and install replacements.
A few years ago, Internet Service Providers were failing
regularly, cutting off email and leaving businesses with
dead addresses. Fortunately, the current trend is to buy
out companies while treating their customers as assets—
and provide a (sometimes painful) path for conversion.
I've had to spend a couple of hours this month clarifying
the changeover from my backup provider to the company
that bought it; fortunately, they had satisfactory answers
to my questions.

As you add systems, and take advantage of the
benefits of integrating them, your costs of support go
up faster than the costs of the systems themselves: every
time you modify one component, you may have to test
and change all the others to keep things working. You
may need to manage more staff and more vendors
to support more technical specialties, which would
ultimately raise your management costs.

And of course you have to be prepared for your
suppliers to have sudden technical problems of their
own that interrupt your services. I lost Internet and email
service in California for a couple of days when my server

was damaged by a hurricane in Connecticut (who would expect a hurricane in Connecticut?), and I had to wait for a transfer to another computer in Texas. Fortunately, Tech Support, based in Canada I believe, was very good about keeping me informed.

Develop Your Information Technology Strategy

You need a Business Strategy First

Your Information Technology strategy is based on your business strategy: it's one step below it.

If you don't already have a business strategy, developing one is a good exercise—but if you're just starting out, don't cast it in stone. As your business picks up, you may find that your customers want something altogether different from your carefully planned products and services.

- For instance, my company was at first intended to sell the really terrific general-purpose image processing and spatial modeling software product I started developing in graduate school, as well as apps it could produce and services it could support. Eventually I learned enough about business to understand that there wasn't a big enough market among organizations that could pay enough to sustain the business. By that time, I was supporting the business by consulting in related areas— which required a totally different strategy.

The three essential components of a business strategy are:

- **Mission:** What the organization is trying to accomplish.

- **Vision:** A brief statement of what you're going to do to accomplish that mission.

- **Goals & objectives:** SMART—Specific, Measurable, Attainable, Relevant and Timely.

Information Technology Strategy

Once you have a business strategy, IT strategy has multiple branches, including:

- Plans to keep the technology supporting your core product/service secure and up-to-date.

- Plans for supporting planned extensions of your offerings.

- Plans for expanding numbers of customers, taking into consideration highly unpredictable growth rates.

- Expanding your skills, automating processes or outsourcing them to make them easier to support.

With luck, these plans can converge somewhat, but will probably result in a set of competing priorities. For instance, extra security precautions like two-factor authentication can make your product a little harder for prospective customers to use, discouraging them from trying it out. Having your plans documented can be helpful when you have to make a quick decision: for instance, should you spend money on higher bandwidth to make your work easier, or save it because the specialized server for your manufacturing equipment could fail at any time?

Define your routine processes

Defining processes is an important step before investing in new Information Technology. Documenting the way you're running your business has additional benefits:

- You're less likely to forget something important, or drop back into less efficient methods.

- You can train someone else quickly when you need to do so suddenly. Or even not suddenly.

- Setting methods down on paper sometimes also shows you where you could be more efficient; for example, two similar steps could be combined to be performed as one.

Make notes about things that are important for you to do and the best ways to go about them. Organize them into a checklist (or set of checklists) so that you don't forget steps. Later, you can look for ways to use software to do some tasks for you, or if you add staff or outsource, you've got a clear explanation of what's needed.

For example:

- Start of day:

   o Check calendar

   o Run backups

     o Run software updates that include possible security fixes

     o Clean up email; respond to urgent messages

     o Note yesterday's contacts with clients & others

     o Start the rest of today's task list

- End of day: Run shutdown process

- Weekly:

     o Set up next week's appointments

     o Follow up on delegated long-term tasks

     o Catch up on technical reading, at least headlines

- Quarterly: Strategic plan review

- Yearly: Tax preparation

Prioritize

You're never going to get everything done that should be done, or protect every bit of data. Identify what's most important in all aspects of your business: tasks, prospective clients, information you've recorded.

Develop simple ways of labeling the priorities so you don't spend a lot of time trying to remember what you decided.

For instance, which data should be encrypted? If you're using it a lot, encryption and decryption costs time and money, but the more sensitive your information is, the higher the value of the extra security.

I prioritize tasks as well, trading off urgency with importance—early morning cleanup isn't as important as client work, but not cleaning up creates a mess fast, so it's generally a higher priority.

Choose Tools

DISCLAIMER: We'll focus on tools that are useful for managing a wide range of organizations, and leave technology that is specialized for few industries or possibly unique to your company (your core competency") in a "black box" that needs to be addressed by potentially massive amounts of specialized information beyond the scope of this book. Here we'll just address technology for the business that encapsulates the black box.

Single/Multiple Vendor Solutions

There's a concern called "vendor lock-in": that is, if you buy too much of your technology from a single vendor, you'll be stuck with them forever, unable to move easily to better products from someone else. For a very small company, I don't think that should be a concern. On the contrary, with a single vendor you also get "one throat to throttle"—if something goes wrong, that entity is clearly responsible, and you aren't stuck with two organizations blaming each other for your problem rather than trying to solve it.

If you do go with multiple vendors, verify that they'll work well together, and at least be able to import and export data that the other can use. At this stage of your company, avoid custom interfaces between systems whenever possible. Otherwise when one company upgrades their software, the upgrade may not be compatible with your interface, and you'll be stuck re-doing it. Simply ignoring the change may not be an option; it might be required to maintain support from the vendor, and more critically it's likely to include security updates that you'll need to defend your systems.

Follow the Crowd

A useful rule of thumb is to look at your competitors and other organizations similar to yours to see what they're using. What's most popular? That's likely to be your best choice:

- The technology might be popular because it's really good.

- With lots of customers and users, that vendor is less likely to go out of business.

- If you run into problems with it, it'll be easier to find someone who's had the same problem and knows how to fix it.

- If you eventually hire someone to run it for you, it'll be easier to find someone who knows how to use it.

Of course, all of the above must be weighed against factors specific to your organization that would call for different technology.

In-House vs. Cloud

Deciding whether to do your work on your local computer or somewhere in the "cloud" is actually an ancient problem in data processing terms. It dates back at least to the 1960s when I worked on both types of systems. The local computer, in the same room where I keypunched the Fortran software and data cards to feed it, was already obsolete with vacuum tubes that blew every 10 minutes, so we had to keep restarting from scratch. The new technology online system used an easier but less sophisticated language called Basic: I punched those programs onto paper tape, ran them through the local terminal, and waited for results. And waited. And waited.

The advantages of using the cloud (like the online system) are:

- Easy maintenance: updates and some upgrades are done for you automatically.

- What you pay is more related to what you actually use, so you may save money on rarely needed operations.

- When you start adding staff, it's easier to add additional capacity.

- Furthermore, you don't have to provide office space to the machinery—or air-conditioning it as it heats up.

Disadvantages include:

• The automatic updates: the way something works may suddenly change without warning, leaving you scrambling to figure out the new procedure.

• Response time (called latency) from the distant computer will be longer, though not necessarily noticeable.

• If there's a failure somewhere on the network, you lose any capabilities that aren't sitting on your local machine.

• Also, for services that are charged by the hour or minute, there's a risk of absentmindedly leaving the meter running with nothing useful happening.

Computer vs. Tablet vs. Smartphone

Smartphones are acquiring more and more of the capabilities of a computer. Which device you use for what purpose is mostly a tradeoff among the capabilities supported by a large screen size, portability, and security. A smartphone is much easier to steal, whereas a full-sized computer is clumsy for a thief to hide and move around, and tends to be kept in a somewhat secure environment. Laptops and tablets are somewhere in between.

Depending on the nature of your work, I'd recommend keeping as little of your intellectual property on the portable device as possible while retaining the capabilities you need on the road. That includes access to information you keep in the cloud—with extra security because of the vulnerability of your device.

IT Management for *Little** Companies
*From one-person shops
to just too small to have
Information Technology staff

Tools I Use

This section describes tools I personally use in my own practice. They are pretty universally useful, but make sure they work with your core technology, regulatory requirements, and business best practices. I personally use the Microsoft Office suite on a PC for most of what I do, not because it's necessarily the best or the cheapest, but because it's what I started with after the earlier vendors went out of business, and I'm too lazy to change. It also has the reputation of being complicated with a lot of unnecessary features, which keeps it interesting for me, but maybe not for other people.

It would be a good idea for you to review competing products to decide which might be better for your specific purposes. I've listed a few in the following sections, not as recommendations, but just to prove that there are alternatives. A web search of the headings should turn up many more, as well as reviews that compare them.

The fastest way to start is to find out what's cheap and popular. As you gain clarity on what you specifically want to do with your software, you've found the initial requirements for what you actually should buy.

Software choice generally drives hardware choice. While many software applications are available on multiple hardware platforms, they may work better on some than others, and you need to make sure that the computer has enough memory, screen size and resolution, speed, and connections for devices you may want to attach.

Word Processor

A word processor not only lets you collect and store detailed information, but lets you use it in a variety of ways. I personally use Microsoft Word, for the reasons mentioned before, but WordPerfect has also been around for a long time, and there are free versions including Google Docs, LibreOffice, and AbiWord.

Fancy Documents

A word processor lets you produce decent-looking letters, contracts, and forms by varying fonts (letter shapes), sizes, colors, etc., as well as add diagrams, pictures, charts, etc. from other sources, like the following:

CERTIFICATE OF ATTENDANCE

IMC USA
SOUTHERN CALIFORNIA CHAPTER

MARKETING ON LINKEDIN AND BEYOND: HOW TO IMPROVE INTER-GENERATIONAL COMMUNICATION IN BUSINESS

JENNIFER BEEVER

The above-named attendee is eligible to receive:

2/3 Continuing Professional Development Point(s)*

Continuing Professional Development Points are required for the Education component of your triennial recertification of your Certified Management Consultant® (CMC®)

MARGARET CHOCK, PhD CMC, CHAPTER PRESIDENT 2016-2017

3/3/2017

CMC® (Certified Management Consultant™) is a registered certification mark awarded by IMC USA, an ISO/IEC 17024 Certifying Body, that represents evidence of the highest Standards of consulting and adherence to the ethical canons of the profession.
* See p. 2

Individualized Documents

Many word processors include a "mail-merge" capability that lets you produce personalized form letters, envelopes, or mailing labels from a list of names, addresses, and other individualized information. I personalize the certificate above for each speaker, meeting topic, and attendee automatically using Word's mail merge. Come to think of it, I should also use mail merge to create the emails for sending it out to the attendees.

Text Editor

A text editor is a very simple form of a word processor, without fancy formatting. If you're already using a word processor you don't need it. However, it can be used to capture information on small or simple devices for which the software of a word processor would be too cumbersome. You can usually transfer information from a text editor to a word processor, but not necessarily vice versa.

Most computer operating systems include a text editor, like Windows Notepad.

Spreadsheet

A spreadsheet is software specialized for handling information in grids or tables of rows and columns. Microsoft Excel is very popular; that's what I use. Google has Google Sheets, Apple has Numbers. There are free versions as well, such as the one included in the WPS Office suite.

Calculations & Graphs

Spreadsheet programs will support arithmetic calculations and in some cases a variety of mathematical functions, both inside of each cell (a unique row/column combination, or "box" on the grid) and among cells.

- For instance, if I label each column to correspond to a particular month, I can sum the total amount in each of my little savings, checking, and investment accounts—each figure provided in its own row—then subtract the current month's sum from last month's to see whether I'm gaining or losing. That's done by entering something like "= Z6 - Y6," where "=" means this following is a calculation, Z6 is column Z row 6 (the cell containing this month's sum), and Y6 is the cell with last month's.

The spreadsheet software may support graphs of various types:

Cumulative Errors - Typical

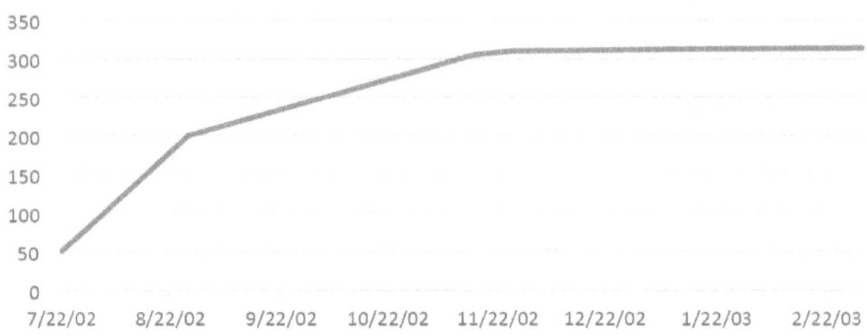

- For one client, I drew a diagram of the normal trend of total software errors you'd expect to find during testing. There'd be a lot at first, then gradually fewer and fewer with each subsequent test. (I've heard a rule of thumb that for every 10 software bugs you fix, you create 3 new ones.)

Total # of issues

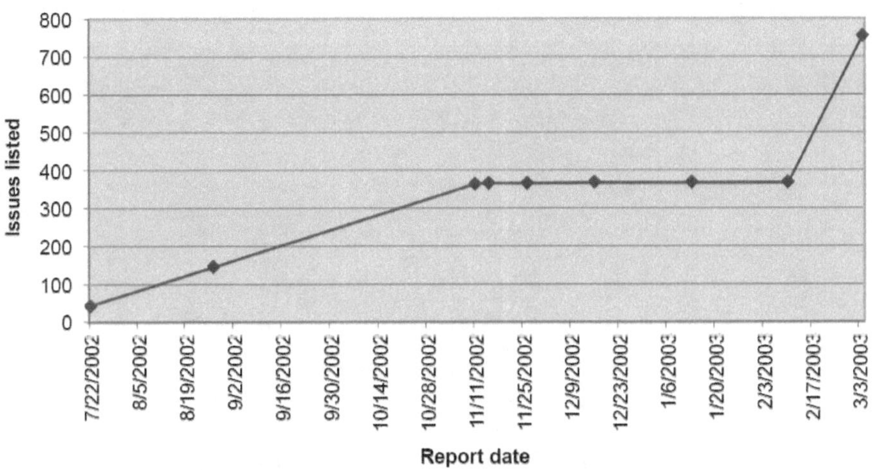

For this client, the trend was as expected... until a year into the project when there was a huge blip—three times the total found so far. Turned out the customers had decided that they really wanted a different vendor's system, and were gaming the error-reporting system to try to get out of paying for all the work that had been done.

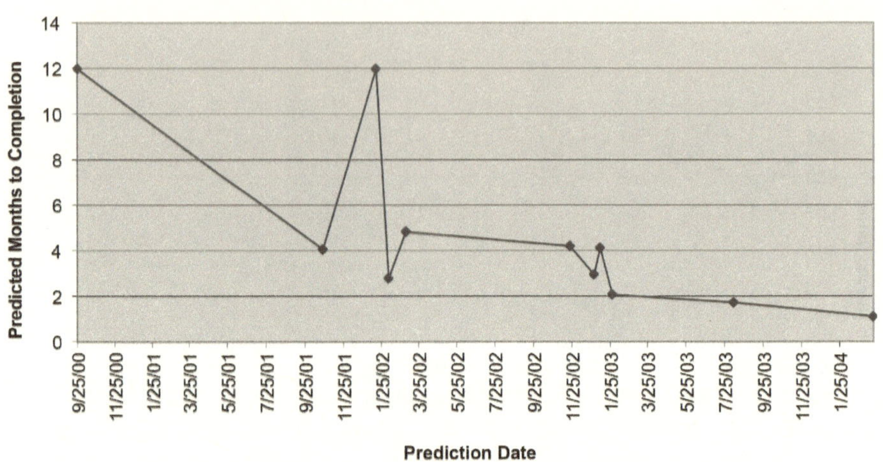

- For another customer, I plotted the promised completion dates vs. percent of modules still not working—a nice (approximately) hyperbolic curve (if you remember your geometry) stretching out to infinity.

Records Management

A spreadsheet with a sorting capability can also be useful for simple records management.

- **Example:** To-do list: Different columns can be used for the start date, due date, urgency, or different categories—then you can, for instance, sort by o Start date (so you can ignore those that don't need to be started yet),

o Urgency (so the top priorities are at the top of the list), and

o Category (so you can work on similar items more efficiently).

Recurring tasks can be relabeled with a new start date when you finish; if they start piling up during the day you can just re-sort to get them out of the way.

• **Example:** Inventory of products, supplies, documents, etc.: sort in columns for "tool type" to find out how many you have, or "location" to find out what's stored at each warehouse.

• **Example:** Contacts—your clients—can be sorted by last name or by company, so you can find Mr. Smith easily, or find out how many people you know at the organization you're visiting tomorrow.

Records Management—Problems with Using a Spreadsheet

However, there's a certain amount of risk to using spreadsheet software for records management. The program is likely to permit you to sort columns independently; one could theoretically, say, sort by last name without including the first name column, leaving you with a useless set of invalid first name-last name combinations if you don't notice in time to undo the sort, or if the software doesn't have an undo function. I've seen that done (I don't think I was the one who did it, but it was a long time ago….). Of course, you will have done your daily backups, so you only have to go through and re-match-up all the records you added or updated today. A database management system is a safer platform, as we'll discuss in the next section.

Another problem with spreadsheet records management is that in order to sort, you have to keep all the data for each person, inventory item, task or the like in a single row. That can get messy.

For instance, in each person's row, you might have a company phone, home phone, cell phone, fax number, or all of the above, as well as two or three email addresses. You might need to know which is which, so you may add a column for each—though you might have to do extra work to find out which column to use, if it matters. As you add more specialized columns, you'll wind up with a lot of blank entries for clients who may not have so much contact information on file. And if there are multiple people at the same company, you'll have a lot of duplicate data as you enter the company address and other information for each of them. Your spreadsheet gets big, unwieldy, and hard to read and manage.

Database Management System

A general-purpose database management system is like a Swiss Army knife for handling all kinds of information. It's a bit more complicated to use than the other tools, but once it's set up it makes your operations much more reliable and efficient. It provides:

- Safer sorting: when you sort by any column, each row stays intact by default.

- Better organization of complicated data.

- Easy data entry.

- Simple statistics.

- Automated lists and reports.

One of the most obvious uses I've found is in setting up contact management systems for my own company and various small nonprofits (though nowadays you might prefer just to buy a professionally designed contact management system, but bear with me for the sake of the example).

Consider the previous example of a spreadsheet of customers, employees, vendors, etc. with columns for first name, last name, company, email, address, etc., in one row for each person—with maybe a general office phone number, direct line, fax number, mobile number, home phone number, etc. etc. The spreadsheet gets wide and unwieldy, even though a lot of those entries may be unused for particular individuals. Using a database management system, you can just add an extra index column to each table, with a unique code for each person—typically just counting the order you put them in, 1, 2, 3, and so on. Then you can add another table just for contact numbers: one column for the number or email address, the second with the index of the person it belongs to, and a third indicating "home," "fax," etc. Then you tell the computer that the contact table's index number is the same as the person index number. When you look up the person in a report or data entry form, you can also see the list of the various ways you can contact them.

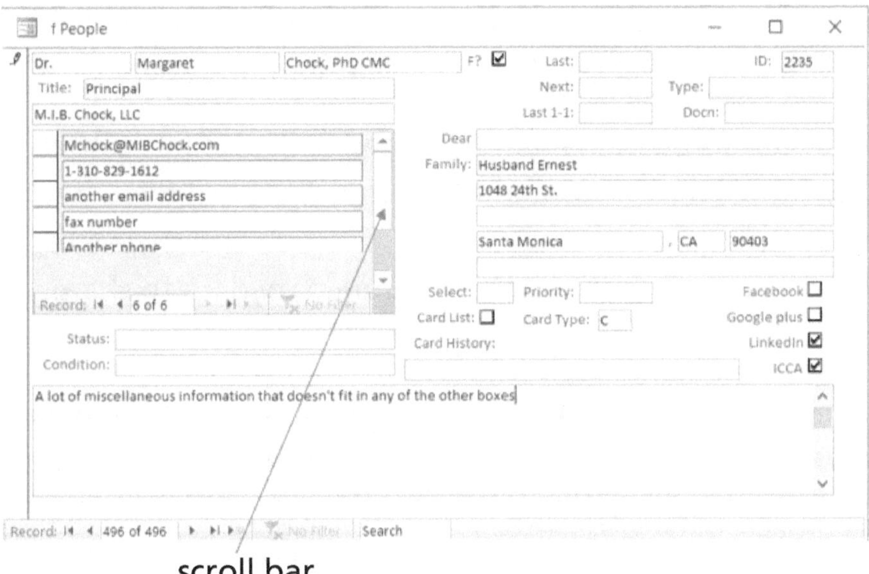

scroll bar

Here's a record from my personal contacts database. I don't recommend the format—it's evolved over the years and I'd design it differently now. The point to notice is the list of email and phone numbers—it has a scroll bar, which indicates that the list doesn't have to fit in the space available; there can be as many items as needed. The underlying list has an index, which isn't visible. The value is 2235 for each of the entries tied to this main record—person #2235 in the database, as shown in the upper right-hand corner.

In the same way, if a number of your contacts belong to the same company or organization, you can split up person-specific information from company-specific information, and tie them together with indexes.

A database management system will also let you set up forms for easy data entry, design standard queries to sort the data and run simple statistics, and generate reports to print out detailed or summary data to share with other people.

The same database management system can support several different applications that might have nothing to do with each other: contact management, inventory, activity tracking, research data, clinical data, product data, you name it. So, you only need to learn how to use a single tool for all of them.

Contact Management System

A contact management system is a database system specialized in managing information about people—customers particularly, but potentially employees, vendors, friends, etc.

It might not be flexible enough to handle other types of data. It might also not be flexible enough to handle exactly the types of information that are important to you. If that's the case, you should make sure it has a large notes or memo field that can be searched by any keywords you choose, to hold the information the designers didn't think you would need.

A contact management system may come integrated with tools beyond the database system to facilitate communication with customers. For instance, a system used by the Institute of Management Consultants supports email to members, newsletter publication, and meeting announcements through a Web interface.

I personally started building contact management systems using database management systems before commercial versions became widespread; I'm running three of them now, including my personal one, which I developed over decades to suit my own needs, and a couple of others specialized for my roles in specific nonprofit organizations.

Commercial versions include SalesForce and numerous inexpensive versions including Zendesk and FreeAgent.

Email & Browser

Everyone has an email address and a World Wide Web browser nowadays. Surely you're using them already!

Website Platform

You'll need a website to establish yourself as a real business. You can start by just copying a free decorative template that lets you type in information, then hiring a developer later on to provide a unique design and nice formatting. A content provider can interview you to develop professional-sounding wording if you don't write well yourself.

A platform that provides an email account with your company address will give you even more credibility.

I started out by building my own using FrontPage (now obsolete), but later hired designers for a fancier format, using DreamWeaver. I worked with a content manager to transfer that to WordPress, which will theoretically be easier to update myself. When I find the time.

Time & Task Tracking

I use Microsoft Outlook's automated task-tracking software, organized by date, time, priority and category, since it's fancier than an old one I'd developed on a database management system. Most tasks repeat or carry over from day to day; as the day's work on each is finished, they can be removed from the list to reappear automatically the next day they're needed.

However, I still carry a paper-based daily reminder—an old-fashioned, pen-and-paper notebook is lighter, more durable, and less likely to be stolen than a smartphone.

And its battery never runs down. It includes the day's appointments, any information that has to be carried around, and 15-minute increments I can record time spent, for later entry in a time-tracking spreadsheet.

Project Management Systems

There are tools to chart lists of tasks and subtasks for a project, the time estimated for each, dependencies between tasks, and people responsible. These are very useful for large, complex projects, though a spreadsheet may be just as useful for simple ones. I started with an (at the time) very sophisticated project management system (Microsoft Project) when I was developing software. More recently, I've used a less-expensive version (Steelray) that reads my clients' project plans, and allows minor edits.

Document Readers / Editors

Data files produced by one software application often can't be understood by another application, or at least are likely to get garbled in translation. If you're faced with a file produced by someone else, you don't necessarily have to buy the same software in order to read it, or even make minor updates. There are cheap or free readers available for most common file formats—for instance, PDF readers for viewing and limited markup of documents ending in ".pdf." You can find such readers online by searching for the suffix (the part at the end after ".") followed by "reader," for instance "xlsx reader" for Excel spreadsheets.

Some research journals require special reading software, which is usually provided free by the publisher once you've paid for the publication.

Presentation Tools

When you're talking to customers, prospects, eventually employees, and other groups, it's useful to have presentation materials ready to be projected on a screen to be visible to a larger group, to illustrate points that need visualization, to reinforce what you're saying, to make things clearer to people who read more easily than listen—and to remind yourself what you're talking about! If they can be printed out automatically, they can serve as review materials for your audience. Some speakers distribute them ahead of time to facilitate note-taking.

PowerPoint gets a lot of disrespect these days, but I don't see what's so different from other products on the market. It's a lot more versatile than the old slideshows I used to use—or even the 8 ½ x 11 transparencies we used to project from a light table! Competitors that are still around include Harvard Graphics and Corel Presentations. Free versions include Google Slides and Keynote.

Graphics—Paint, Photo, Visio

To expand the capabilities of your presentation software, and provide illustrations of your internal processes, specialized drawing and photograph manipulation tools are useful. Some may come with the operating system (Windows Paint and Photos). I also use computer-aided design (CAD) software (Visio, in this case) that in its most basic form draws labeled boxes, and connects them with lines that stay attached when I move the boxes around. That's been useful for flowcharts, organization charts, diagrams of networks of various types, floor plans, etc., as in the following example illustrating problems leading to a lawsuit on which I consulted:

IT Management for *Little** Companies
*From one-person shops
to just too small to have
Information Technology staff

Actual Information Flows (total number of software versions and requirement changes increases as time goes on, multiplying changes that need to be managed by both software development and data conversion)

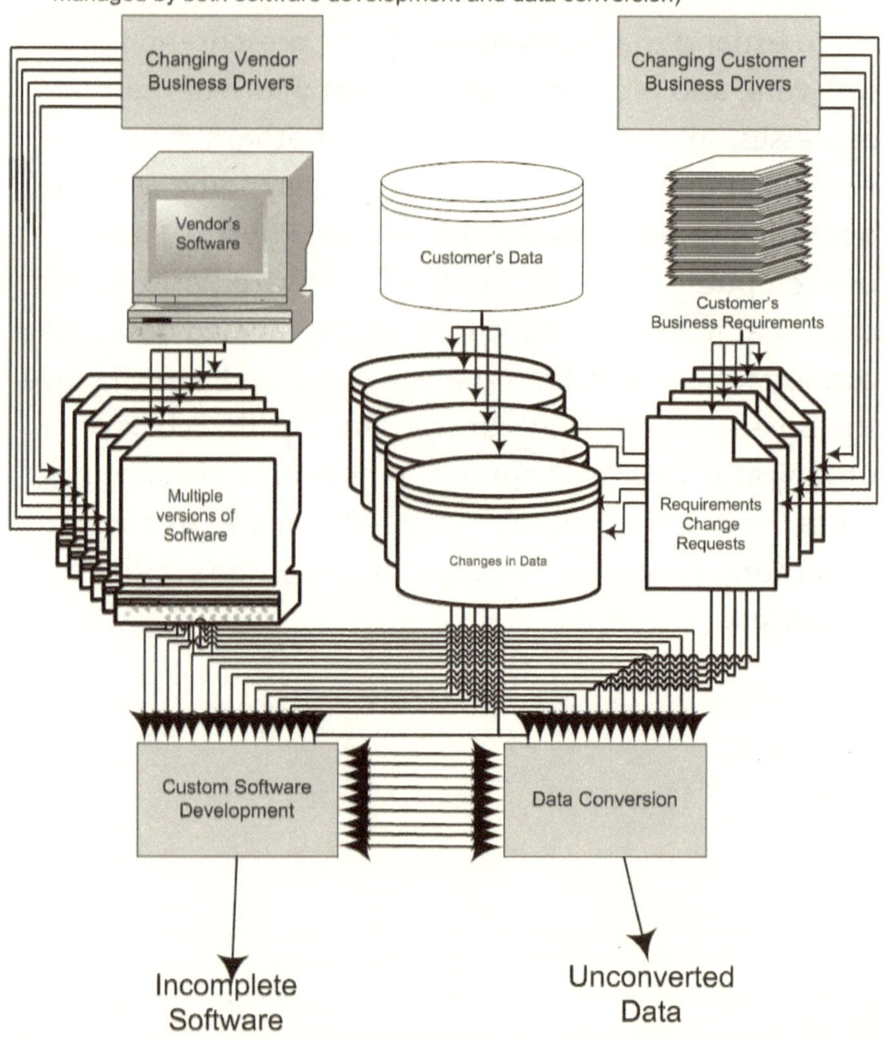

As You Add Staff

Once you add an employee, or a contractor who will work with you on your computer systems, management of those systems starts getting a lot more complicated. Here are some suggestions for integrating people into your technology.

Start Defining Processes

As you add staff, make your daily procedure checklists available in case you take sick or, after a few years, risk taking a vacation. Expand them as necessary, first with the reason the process is needed, then with definitions, scripts, illustrations, location of the vendor's service manual, etc. Formalize who will do what, documenting handoffs. Flowchart software is helpful to illustrate what's going on.

And yes, processes are part of Information Technology Management! I was once asked to develop inventory software for a chemistry research lab. We started by documenting the current inventory management process, and compared it to the workflow of an automated system. We demonstrated that in the automated system, every time the chemists used a reagent they'd have to stop and enter at least the type of reagent and the quantity into the computer, rather than just eyeballing the bottle to see whether they needed to re-order. Realizing that the new system would be more work than the old one, the chemists abandoned the idea.

Especially if you've hired an employee, there's suddenly more government-required paperwork to manage—defined processes can ensure you don't forget steps or delay them too long. I found that my part-time employee was spending about a third of her time on handling the required employee paperwork—that was critical overhead to be delegated and automated as fast as possible.

Capture & Preserve Data

Train your staff to document what they're doing as well: checklists for the procedures they perform, guides to where the data they use is kept, anything else that someone taking over their job in an emergency would need to know. Make sure you understand each other's procedure documentation before more people (complications) get added to the mix.

Expand your backup system to include everyone, preferably on an automatic basis so you don't have to rely on each staff member—or at least put one individual in charge of making sure backup gets done.

Teach Paranoia

Teach your staff to be as paranoid as you are, and to remember that competitors and other thieves are out to attack your little community!

Define what falls under the umbrella of your organization's intellectual property, and other information that you're legally, contractually, and/or morally required to protect. Explain to your staff what it is, and why.

Put boundaries on communicating with friends outside the organization:

- Don't share confidential company information...

- And don't ask questions that could reveal it.

Cybersecurity should be a major consideration when you shape your internal processes. Bring in a certified cybersecurity professional at least annually to evaluate your organization, help you put as much protection as feasible into place, and train your staff.

Internal Threats

Your contractors and even your own employees need supervision to make sure they don't leak data or compromise your systems.

They might email important documents to their home accounts or carry them away on thumb drives, DVDs, or laptops. They may just intend to do extra work for you at home—or may plan to sell the information to competitors. Even if their intentions are good, once the information goes out in the world, it can easily be stolen.

Angry employees, perhaps just fired or laid off, can damage critical systems before they leave.

Even happy workers can be risky. My first experience with a hacker (the definition used by IT people—someone who tries to find out how a system works using not-necessarily-authorized methods) was a sweet little gray-haired lady who finally got barred from using the church computer because she was curious, and kept fiddling with the system after repeated warnings.

And one of the nicest guys I ever worked with disappeared suddenly one afternoon, reportedly marched out of the facility by two security guards. He was the expert on the innards of our ancient legacy mainframe. Rumor was that he'd been fiddling with the system so that it never quite worked right, so that he'd always be indispensable.

So keep an extra eye on things, and take your cybersecurity auditor's advice.

Classify your data

To be effective in protecting your data, distinguish what needs to be available to whom, to apply the strongest protection to the most critical data, but make sure that everyone who needs to use it can access it.

A standard tool for organizing this information is CRUD Matrix: a list of all relevant people, with checkoff columns for who has permission to Create, Read, Update and Delete it. For example:

	CEO	Admin	Finance	Sales & Marketing	Operations
Personal Data	CRUD	CRUD	CRUD	CRUD	CRUD
Employee Records	R	R	CRUD		R
Financial Statements	R		CRUD		
Customer Information	CR	CRU	R	CRUD	
Product Information	CR		R	R	CRUD

Everybody gets control of his or her own set of personal data. The **CEO** can look at everything else in the system, but delegates actual manipulation of the data other than adding customers or product ideas for follow-up by Sales & Marketing or Operations respectively. The Administrator needs to see employee contact information, and sometimes receives phone calls with information about prospective customers, to be forwarded to Sales & Marketing. Finance needs to see some information from all departments, and in this case oversees Human Resources. Sales & Marketing manages customer data, and needs to know what's going on with the company's products. Operations handles product information, and needs some information about Operations employees.

"Read" is not so important in a very small organization; it's too hard to keep secrets yet. And "Create" may be pretty obvious—it depends on individual responsibilities. But the people who are allowed to "Update" and "Delete" need to be clearly defined up front. At this point you need procedures to make sure you don't step on each other's toes.

Of course, if your organization is small enough it will turn out that everyone needs access to everything, but discussion of access limits might at least lead to some initial compromises: who agrees to notify whom before doing what, and how. Such agreements set the stage for formalizing these methods later on.

Most systems allow you to set access permissions at this level, to automate identifiers for each person (client, customer, vendor, investor, business prospect, employee) or interfacing computer system to restrict what they can do. Make sure the system is easy to manage, because who needs to be able to do what can change suddenly.

Take Inventory

Clients have been amazed when I added up all the components and systems they'd collected over the years.

For instance, I was brought in to manage IT for a little research laboratory. One of my first projects was to find out exactly what kind and quantity of technology they were using. I traced their network—it turned out everything was running off the Internet, with no security for their valuable research. Their backup server was a little device up on a shelf in the telephone closet (which would have fallen off in the mildest earthquake). Its capacity was too small for all the computers it was supposed to be backing up—but that didn't matter since it apparently hadn't been working for months. The facilities manager, who had been more or less in charge, was amazed at the total number of devices I turned up.

The ancients among you might remember the Year 2000 (Y2K) Panic mentioned a couple of times earlier. Computer systems all over the world were expected to go haywire, since up to that point the oldest, most critical systems had used two digits for years to save space. When '99 rolled over to '00, date calculations would fall off a cliff and create chaos in the rest of the software. Fortunately, most major companies spent months tracking down and fixing their date calculations ahead of time, and not much went wrong.

At the time, I was working for a company of about 500 people, and was tasked with taking inventory of just the critical business systems to research and repair; the rest could be retired or replaced later if necessary. We finally got it down to 72 independent "critical" business systems. A large percentage of them had been previously unknown to the Information Technology Department. And that didn't include all the technical systems used for product design and development—all of those were somebody else's responsibility!

So try to keep track of what systems your company has accumulated. Each is a source of potential trouble and expense, including cybersecurity failures (if your annual audit misses them), potential duplications of effort, missed opportunities for data sharing, and holes in your operation if the only person who understands the system leaves your organization.

Hardware

Once you've added staff, the underlying hardware starts getting complicated: you'll likely need internal computer networks and phone systems. Find reliable local support services to keep the systems working. A good vendor should be able to recommend what you need, though keep in mind that even the best has a built-in bias towards bigger, more complicated systems that will provide more business for them.

But don't stint on hardware quality and capacity; your main costs will be in staff time. Make sure your local hardware (or your cloud contract) will keep them busy, not twiddling their thumbs waiting for a response from the computer. Also, get advice on what you'll need if your business grows suddenly—make sure your current investment can be part of a more powerful system later, so that you won't have to throw everything out and start from scratch.

Compatibility

New staff members may bring favorite business tools with them. To the extent that they'll be working independently that may not be a problem, but, once they need to share data, you might need to set an organizational standard. An easy way to do that is to choose whatever is most popular—it will be easier to find staff you won't have to train to use it.

The tools that your staff is using need to work together smoothly. In some cases, it might be enough to be able to transfer data from one machine to another and have it be understood, but in other cases you might need to start restricting the tools used, or face complicated programming to translate the data to work with different systems.

For a while I had a nice stream of business figuring out how to translate the formats of new geographic information systems (GIS) to each other. Eventually most companies settled on a standard for exporting and importing at least the basic geometry data, though often there was extra useful information in the first system that the second one couldn't handle, and had to be discarded or managed separately.

To avoid such problems, add new systems as gradually as possible and integrate them with the ones you already have. The costs won't just be additive; there's a cost for increasing complexity for interfaces between systems and multiple technologies.

In-Person vs. Virtual Team; In-House Social Media

Traditionally a company would start adding staff in one location—a garage or small office, or meeting at a local coffee shop. You'd talk to each other directly, all looking at the same document.

Now even very small companies can start virtually, meeting each other online, even working out of different cities. Combinations of videoconferencing, online bulletin boards and social media can allow your staff to form teams for different purposes, communicating as a group and posting documents specific to the job at hand informally.

Tools are available to allow teams to work on the same document at the same time: these are called Document Management Systems, or Configuration Management Systems, which may include software under development and other assets. That would drive me crazy, personally. However, I have found markup tools, used on files emailed or traded in an online repository, very useful as long as some sort of check-out procedure is used to make sure that team members aren't making simultaneous inconsistent changes. The tools I've used weren't quite good enough—every once in a while, a team member picked up an out-of-date version to work on. I never did, of course.

In this sort of distributed environment, cybersecurity and protection of trade secrets become trickier to ensure. Make sure your security expert evaluates what you're doing—very carefully!

Getting Outside Help

As your technology starts evolving beyond what you and your non-tech staff can handle yourselves, but before you start hiring full-time technical help, look to vendors who can work alongside you.

An information technology consultant can look at your processes and recommend ways to make them more efficient and automate them (though you might want to hire a general business consultant first to make sure you have the right processes)! The consultant can help you develop a set of technical requirements. Make sure these requirements are prioritized, so that the most important ones will be developed first.

Your best bet is to select systems that are designed to do most of what you want, with minor adjustments to your existing ways of doing business. Avoid customization where possible. Customization is expensive in the first place, and every time the vendor upgrades its product, the custom work needs to be retested to make sure it still works. And if the vendor decides to head in another direction, the customization may need to be done all over again from square one.

Choose vendors you'll want to work with for a long time, and build good relationships with them, so that they'll be cooperative with training, troubleshooting— and remembering your custom requirements as they do further development. Once you get started, technology requires maintenance forever. Software fixes and upgrades obsolete hardware; then hardware modifications make software obsolete—but you need to keep upgrading just to keep ahead of the newest cybersecurity threats, let alone business growth.

There's a lot of concern about getting "locked in" to a particular vendor's structure and unique capabilities when acquiring multiple tools, risking large amounts of retraining for you and your staff to switch to another supplier. On the other hand, for a small organization with no IT staff, there's a big advantage: the products will (usually) work together smoothly, and you can make the vendor fix them if they don't. If you use some systems that are incompatible with others, however, and you hit an issue, you might have a hard time getting a vendor's attention to address your problem. Each will be sure that the other is at fault.

For critical systems, make sure you have protection against vendors going out of business. Choose suppliers that are so popular that if they fail, someone else will want to take over and support their customers. For any customized software, set up an escrow arrangement that will ensure access if the vendor does fail, or is unable to continue support.

Always keep an eye on changes in technology (or make sure someone else is doing so for you) so that you'll have contingency plans for dealing with the volatile environment. As a small organization you can't expect disruption to respect your convenience, so know what to do (a written plan is valuable) if your systems become temporarily unavailable or permanently so.

IT Management for *Little** Companies
*From one-person shops
to just too small to have
Information Technology staff

In Conclusion

So take advantage of the wonderful support tools computer systems can provide to even very small organizations. Follow the crowd when making choices that don't directly impact your core capabilities. Set up defensive perimeters to protect your company and check them frequently as threats change.

And I can't stress this enough: back up your data. Way offsite!

IT Management for *Little** Companies
*From one-person shops
to just too small to have
Information Technology staff

Acknowledgements

Thank you very much to Emerson Books editors Elena Petricone and Chloe Lizotte for insisting that the book had to be intelligible to readers, and providing translations where I couldn't figure that out, as well as patiently digging out the grammatical errors that had hidden themselves so carefully. Thank you Cindy Murphy of Bluemoon Graphics for finding a great cover and resolving some rather tricky design problems. And thank you Ken Lizotte for your encouragement, and for putting together such a great team!

And especially thank you to Dr. Ernest P. Chock for support, comfort, preliminary edits, and brownies!

IT Management for *Little** Companies
*From one-person shops
to just too small to have
Information Technology staff